THE POLLEN

Ray D

To Stephen & Lorraine

Illustrated by Philip McGuinness

With all good wishes

Ray Davey

The Corrymeela Press

Dedicated to our grandchildren

Andrew, Patrick, Kate,
Charlotte, Raymond , Peter,
Patrick, Caitlin & Christopher.

and
the Corrymeela "family" of the last 25 years.

The Pollen of Peace

ISBN: 1 873739 00 1
This edition published June 1991 by Corrymeela Press.
Copyright © 1991 Ray Davey.
All proceeds of this edition will go to the Corrymeela Community.

Designed and Printed by Express Litho Limited, Belfast.

1

Foreword

This little book began when Robert, my older son, suggested that I should write up some of my experiences at different periods of my life, especially over the last 25 years of Corrymeela. At first I played with the idea and then at the beginning of September 1990, I ruptured an Achilles tendon and found myself with a lot of time on hand. So, with the help of a word processor supplied by Roger Curry, my son-in-law, I started.

I found this to be excellent occupational therapy and it has made me more convinced that the short story or word picture is one of the best ways of communicating one's thoughts. After all it has the highest authority of all. So gradually the ideas and memories came back and I tried to put them on paper. I have used quite a few that I had written for Corrymeela worships, and there the listeners included a wide circle of people from children to adults, and in setting them out I have not tried to classify them, in the belief that a story or incident can appeal to any group.

For the most part they are personal experiences and have a Corrymeela setting or theme. In them I have tried to express my own outlook at this stage of my life; my gratitude for all I have received; the friendships and the experiences in addition to the unfinished agenda and challenges of today and the hopes for whatever lies ahead in the future. Above all that ever deepening sense that we are in Surer Hands than our own, as we so often sing at Corrymeela: "He's got you and me brother (or sister) in His hand".

Many have taken part in the production of this book.

Alan Evans of Express Litho Limited has been an inspiration to work with and his experience and expertise have been invaluable.

Philip McGuinness's illustrations have added much to the text.

Once again I am in debt to Alf McCreary for his friendship and for writing the introduction.

Thanks also to Roger Courtney for permission to use the title of his famous song.

To Christiana Spengler of Halle in Germany for her lovely silhouette drawing used in the cover.

My debt to Kathleen, my wife, is unlimited. Not only for her patience and skill in proof reading, in making many important suggestions and for the multitude of times she has lifted my sagging morale.

I hope some of the stories may be of use in schools, youth and peace groups and churches as well as in private reading. What I have written is a small attempt to express my gratitude for Corrymeela, its Members, Friends and young people and all they have given us over the last 25 years. All profits from the book will be devoted to the work of the Community.

Ray Davey

Introduction

Anyone who knows Ray Davey will hear the gentle wisdom of this visionary yet self-effacing man coming through every line of this volume. Those who have not yet made his acquaintance will discover a thoughtful guide and friend, in these quiet but spiritually-charged observations from a life that has been rich and well-lived.

Ray Davey's many friends each have their special picture of him. Many years ago, as a student at Queen's, I met Dr Davey who was then the Presbyterian Chaplain at the University. Despite my reservations, at that time, about religion in general and Presbyterianism in particular, Ray had (and still has) the compelling quality of making goodness seem attractive. By simply being himself, he made more converts to the faith than he will ever know.

This early friendship matured down the years, like those with many others whose lives were touched by Ray and his lovingly indispensable partner Kathleen. Sometimes it was the gift of a special book or a word in a corner of Queen's or Corrymeela which made all the difference. As always his wisdom and spiritual strength were expressed quietly - no flamboyant statements or histrionics, but the down-to-earth observations of a man who lives and understands community and Christianity at their best.

This collection of writings might be termed "an anthology of Thought for the Day". Each article has its spirituality cloaked in the reality of so many ordinary, and extraordinary, things all around us - the smile of a child, the beauty of the sea, the humble example of a pet, the forgiveness arising from the agony of war, the gracious strength of a Mother Teresa. The story is told of the composer Sir Edward Elgar who pencilled on the score of Nimrod, from his Enigma Variations, "This is the best of me". This late-flowering is arguably the best of Ray Davey. It has been a privilege to treasure the friendship of such a man, and to savour the beauty and wisdom of such a book.

Alf McCreary
Belfast, May 1991.

Contents

The Soldier v. The Artist

It was the end of June 1942 and we had been captured in the fall of Tobruk in North Africa. Then followed a long and tedious journey across the desert with many stops and starts. Finally we had crossed the Mediterranean Sea and arrived at Lecce, on the East Coast of the "toe" of Italy. We were still adjusting to the new life and wondering what the future held in store for us. As we were escorted through the streets of the town a great number of the locals came out to look us over. One of our number felt that we should make some response and began to sing the song that was very popular at home in the early years of the war: "There'll always be an England". There was little or no response from the people. Almost certainly they did not understand English, but I remember one woman did throw a rose to one of the prisoners.

Shortly after, we were marched into a large school and divided up into groups of some 60 prisoners and placed in different class rooms under a fully armed guard, in case anyone wanted to make an escape move. The arrival of the rations diverted attention from such things and we each received what seemed to be an outsize dog-biscuit, which we softened in water and gratefully ate.

After this interlude we all squatted down as best we could to relax. Then one of the prisoners began to play a mouth-organ he had managed to hold on to in the many searches we had gone through. Casually he began to play, which he could do very well.

First he played all the well known war time songs: "Pack up your troubles" and so on. His selection subtly changed, as he launched into well known Italian Opera, which he knew. We had "La donna e mobile" and "O sola meo". Enthusiasm among the captive audience mounted. It was an amazing study to watch our young Italian guard. At first he had been grim and stiff, then slowly the change had begun to take place. His face relaxed and then his feet began to tap to the rhythm of the music.

Suddenly it all happened. Our musician knew his Italian Opera and also how every Italian longed to be another Gigli, or a second Caruso. Our guard smiled gently then took his rifle from his shoulder, loosened his army tunic and clearing his throat began to sing. His first piece was from Carmen: The Toreador's Song. This was greeted with tumultuous applause and instant calls for an encore. Following next came: "E lucevan le stille" from Tosca. The performance continued for a long time and at length it came to an end. This was greeted with a mighty standing ovation.

He bowed all round with a very happy smile, then slowly his tunic was adjusted and his cap put on and finally he took up his rifle again and slung it across his shoulder. The performance was over but for all of us the memory lingered on. Things after that, however, were never quite the same again. We had yet many ordeals to pass through, but that experience remained to lift our hearts from time to time. We came to realise that there were those timeless things that transcend our differences and bind us together into one common humanity.

A Stowaway

Away back in 1953 I had to travel to America and sailed from Liverpool to New York on the liner 'Brittanic'. For the first day or two it was an interesting experience but after that it became rather boring and monotonous, just ploughing through the waves, no land in sight, the steady drone of the engines hour after hour, and of course eating and sleeping.

One morning, however, as we were sitting watching the waves go by, there was quite a stir of excitement as we spotted another liner sailing in the opposite direction. First of all it was just a small spot on the horizon and we saw it grow nearer and nearer. We were told it was the 'Mauretania". Its course was set in our direction and we looked forward to having a good close-up view of it, and indeed some passengers rushed away below to fetch their cameras. Suddenly about 11 o'clock things began to happen. First we heard the steady beat of the engines slacken and the ship started to slow down. Next, as the 'Mauretania' drew closer to us, there was a rumbling noise, as one of our life boats was lowered down to sea level. This naturally raised a great buzz of excitement and speculation as to the cause. We knew that it was a very expensive business to stop two liners in mid Atlantic, so it must be very serious.

Soon we had the answer, as a young fair haired woman was escorted down a ladder into the life-boat. Believe it or not she was a stowaway. She wanted to leave her home in England to go and live in America. She was running away from her home and going to live in another country.

That, of course, is a very old story and yet a very modern one, as we are reminded so often on our television screens about the number of young people who leave home for the big cities. There is, of course, all the difference in the world between leaving home and running away from home. The crucial point is why young people leave home. We find it right at the beginning of the Bible, when Adam and Eve try to run away from God by hiding themselves among the trees of the garden. They were very conscious that they had disobeyed God. So later on with Jonah, because of his disobedience. Of course the classic story is of the Prodigal Son and his escape into the Far Country. I would say that there were two reasons for this and they were closely connected. On the one hand he did not understand himself, or who he was or what he wanted and he believed that getting away from home would solve all his problems. In addition he did not understand his father and the sort of person he really was. Then when

9

he got away from home he began to see himself in a new light with all his false ideas and illusions. In fact 'he came to himself' and at the same time began to understand the sort of person his father was. In short he saw who he really was, where he belonged and what he was made for.

St. Augustine who had been a prodigal himself put it all in a sentence: "You have made us for yourself and our hearts are restless till they find their rest in you".

Incredible News

It was June 6th 1944. I was a prisoner-of-war in Dresden in East Germany. As a YMCA Field Worker and also a minister, I was permitted to travel round the various work-camps for Allied prisoners in the city and surrounding district. My task was to be a pastor to the men in these camps, conducting occasional services and giving whatever help was possible to those in need. I was always escorted by an armed German soldier. On this particular day I was due to visit a camp in a suburb called Radeburg about 10 kilometres out of the city. The prisoners were billeted in huts just a short distance from the brick factory where they worked. We arrived in the late noon after a long walk on the hot dusty road.

Slowly the men began to trickle back in twos and threes from the factory. You could see the weariness in their eyes and faces with so many hardships to endure and so many disappointments. Some had been prisoners for 4 years and had children growing up that they had never seen. Then there was the ever present reality of forced labour, confinement, restrictions and at times fear and uncertainty about what lay ahead and the welfare of loved ones at home. As they sat around and chatted, preparing for a shower and a meal of whatever was available, there was a bit of commotion at the door and a prisoner pushed his way through. We could see that he was so breathless with excitement that he could hardly speak. It came out in gasps: "Boys it's happened--The Allies have landed in Normandy--The bridgehead is holding and the advance has begun".

It is difficult to describe the scenes as more and more prisoners arrived. The release of pent up feelings and emotions that had been held back for years: the cheers - the hugs - the shouts - the songs. Of course we were not safe nor free yet, there remained so much to be done over the next 10 months. But the Allies had landed, the crucial battle had been won. Freedom, home, a new life and loved ones were in sight.

I still find it difficult even after such a long time to tell that story without being moved. It was one of the high moments of my life. Suddenly a new future opened up before us and the frustration, anxiety and monotony of the present was about to pass away. I always think of it as a marvellous parable of the Christian Hope that lies ahead. There we were languishing in German captivity. Then D-Day came, the Forces of liberation had landed and the crucial battle won and the bridgehead established and the enemy in principle defeated. True the war was not over yet, and we were still captives, but sooner or later the day would come and the victory be completed.

I am sure the early disciples must have felt rather as we did on that late afternoon in 1944, when they met in the Upper Room after the Resurrection. The events they had seen marked the beginning of the end of the old order of evil and pride. The Kingdom of love has been established, but still there is resistance and opposition, but one day it will be fully and completely here and so we pray: "Your Kingdom Come".

Driving In The Fast Lane

David Sheppard captained the English cricket team on many occasions and into the bargain was opening batsman. When I was talking to him recently, I asked if having to open the innings was not the most nerve-racking role in all sport, especially when facing the terrifying speed and power of the West Indian fast bowlers. He acknowledged that it was a very testing experience. Then I asked him what he said to himself in such a situation. He replied: "Well I simply grit my teeth and say to myself that this chap would soon get tired and have to take a rest". Of course the trouble was that there were always two or three other bowlers of similar calibre waiting to take over. David Sheppard is, of course, Anglican Bishop of Liverpool. He had come over to take part in a dialogue with the Catholic Archbishop of Liverpool, Derek Worlock. In the meeting in Queen's University organised by the Corrymeela Community, the subject of their dialogue was "Better Together" in which they spoke of Liverpool and its problems. Indeed it is a city that has much in common with Belfast.

Perhaps it was his training as Opening Batsman that explains the role he has played in his clerical career. He has certainly never taken the easy way nor the soft option. He founded the Mayflower Centre in the East End of London, then he became Bishop of Woolwich and later of Liverpool. For many years he has been outspoken in condemning the injustices and poverty in the inner cities of this country. His last book "Bias to the Poor" and also his famous

Dimbleby lecture on television in 1984, spoke very clearly about the injustice of the two Britains that have emerged. He quoted Gandhi, who, when asked what was his greatest disappointment said "the hard-heartedness of educated people". Unlike so many of his contemporaries David Sheppard has never been afraid to take risks, perhaps another legacy of his cricketing days.

The most recent risk he has taken is with the leader of the Catholic Community in Liverpool, Archbishop Worlock, and, as we have seen, in working together and speaking together on the vast number of social and political issues that touch everybody in the community, irrespective of religion or party. As a result, their concern for these things has given a new credibility, not only to the ecumenical spirit, but also to the church, as being concerned with the whole of life in Liverpool. Three things deeply impressed those of us who heard them speak and talked with them.

In the first place it was very obvious that the two of them had a very Surely that is an all important point for any new venture. In the second place both of them reminded us again and again that the Gospel is not something apart from the rest of life, but to do with all of it: the terrible football tragedy at Hillsborough a few months ago; the closure of the Tate and Lyle factory; the inner city violence at Toxteth, just as much as with services, vigils and Bible study groups. Thirdly, while both were deeply involved with the needs of society, it was obvious that they were both men of deep spirituality and prayer.

Marconi

There are many very intersting stories about Ballycastle, none more so than that of Marconi, the man who gave the whole system of radio transmission to the world. Marconi and his assistant Kemp set up their experimental base in a coal yard just behind the harbour. Then it was in July 1898 that they received a series of V's from Rathlin four miles off shore. This was the first time radio telegraphy had been used successfully for transmitting messages and was very soon to revolutionise the whole system of directing shipping.

Their experiment was very rapidly put into practical and commercial use. The link between Rathlin and Ballycastle was commissioned by no less that Lloyd's, to relay sighting reports of inbound and outbound ships, passing north of the island to their mainland station at Torr Head for onward telegraphic transmission. This had vast advantages over the flag systems previously used, which were obviously of little or no use in fog or mist.

Of course there are many stories about Marconi and it is difficult to know which are true, so I was very pleased to meet a very old lady, Elizabeth Hunter, who had been alive at the time. In fact her father owned one of the hotels, known then as Hunter's Hotel, and it was here that Marconi and Kemp stayed, when they were making their experiments down at the Harbour. By the way, that is where today you will find the most unusual monument dedicated to Marconi and erected in 1978.

Marconi was not there very often but Elizabeth Hunter got to know Kemp very well. She was learning to play the piano and had to practice each evening. Kemp was a very keen fiddler and used to come along when she was playing the piano and began to play with her. They got so enthusiastic that they carried on playing until it was very late and Mr Hunter who would be trying to sleep in the room above, would hammer the floor and tell them to go to bed.

Marconi with Kemp revolutionised the whole idea of communication. Think of what this has meant throughout the world - the messages and the news that are flashed round the continents in a few seconds, how we can talk with our friends in Australia and elsewhere. Then with satellites how live pictures enable us to see things at the ends of the earth as they are actually happening. A great break-through in communication!

I often think that it is remarkable that this miracle of communication started here in Ballycastle, because communication is also Corrymeela's business. Our reason for existing is also to help people to communicate with each other, listening as well as speaking, because this is how understanding, trust and change begin. That to us is the challenge of Marconi, for it is when we learn to talk together that we learn to live together.

Does it not seem strange:-

we have learned to sail across the seas,
we have learned to fly around the earth,
we have learned to rocket to the moon,
but we have yet to learn to walk the earth in peace?

Meeting A Royal In Jerusalem

I will never forget the thrill I had when I first visited Jerusalem. It was summer 1941 and I was on leave from the Egyptian Desert after almost a year there, and now as the train smoothly glided across the landscape, I began to see how right the Biblical writers were to talk of "the land flowing with milk and honey". For after we turned inland at Lydda, the monotonous desert wastes were replaced by patches of cultivated green with trees and small colourful villages, as well as water flowing down the narrow valleys. There away ahead were the hills around Mount Sion. As the train swept on its way, there were glimpses of Bedouin shepherds leading their flocks of sheep, both black and white, as well as goats. At railway crossings camels with their heads in the air cynically watched us rush past. The hillsides were terraced for vines and olives.

It seemed almost to be irreverent to have a Central Station in the Holy City, but it was soon forgotten, as we passed through the Damascus Gate into a very different world that seemingly had changed little in 2000 years. This is what I wrote in the diary I kept: "Down into the little narrow crowded streets, rubbing shoulders with those who seemed to step right out to the Bible, Arabs with red Fezs and long flowing robes, water carriers bent under the weight of their burden, but standing aside to let laden camels pass, Orthodox Jews with their flowing beards and wide brimmed black hats, women gracefully picking their way through the crowds, while bearing water pots on their heads. We passed through these steep narrow streets where no vehicles could go, and the tall houses along the way were so close that they almost seemed to shake hands. There were shops of all description with their wares displayed outside on the street. Moslem, Jew and Christian all mingle here in this seething mass of humanity. What a place for intrigue and treachery!"

Time for us was short so we hastened round the Temple Area, the Via Dolorosa, the Wailing Wall, Gordon's Calvary and so many other places. One trip comes specially to mind. It was away down to the old City of David, through the Valley of Kedron and past the Mount of Olives. It was a scorching day in August and we had taken a taxi down into this valley. We stayed there for about an hour and when we returned we discovered that our taxi was gone. The idea of a two mile walk uphill back to the American YMCA did not appeal to us. Looking round, I saw an estate car with an officer, a Greek Orthodox priest and two soldiers, and they seemed to be preparing to leave. So I hastened over to the officer and asked if there was any chance of a lift. Very graciously he agreed and told us to get into the rear seats with the two soldiers. As we motored up the hill, I noticed from his uniform that the officer was also Greek but I was not sure of his rank. I turned to one of the soldiers and asked about this and he told me that he was the Crown Prince of Greece, and the Priest beside him was the Greek Prime Minister in exile. By the time we arrived back at the King David Hotel, close to the YMCA, I had sufficiently recovered from my surprise to give him a sort of military salute by way of thanks. Whenever I recall that day in Jerusalem, I think of those other surpises the City had, when the Messiah himself came.

I leave it to George MacLeod to express something of what I felt:

It is so wonderful to know of your Incarnation
That you really came in the flesh,
Have walked where we walk,
Have felt what we feel:
And that time and again you could not get away to pray
Because of the pressures of every day.
It is wonderful to know that you came that we might find you
In the pressure of life;
We are released that you are with us this day.

The Two Faces Of Ireland

Sometimes at Corrymeela we get one of those almost perfect days when the sky is blue, the sea shining in the sun and the visibility limpidly clear. On such a day I like to stroll across the front lawn and look out across the Moyle waters to Rathlin and beyond to Jura, and East to the Mull of Kintyre. What a panorama of colour, life and movement. In such a mood it all seems to me like a great stage across which so many ships have passed through the centuries.

Away back in the 5th Century the Vikings came in their long boats to plunder, capture and kill. Moving on to the 16th Century mighty Spanish galleons passed by after the disaster of the Armada. A very vivid reminder of those days is found at Lacada Point off the Giant's Causeway, where the wreck of the Gerona lies. On into the 18th and 19th Centuries many ships sailed from these shores bound for the United States in the hope of a better and freer life there. Some were driven out by religious persecution and others by the horrors of the Potato Famine. Again the HMS Drake from the First World War lies as a wreck in Rathlin's Church Bay. All these ships passing by here spoke of violence, fear, exile, persecution and destruction.

Look again at this great stage, for other ships have passed by here on a very different mission. We think of Patrick who must have known these parts well on his travels through Ireland telling of the One who came as the Prince of Peace. Every time I pass along the road to Belfast I look out for Slemish with its unusual profile, and remember what he did for Ireland so long ago. I recall the poem "Wind over Slemish" from the pen of one of our Corrymeela members, Ted Gordon:-

And except the wind of the spirit
Bear you, Patrick, with your feet shod with the Gospel,
Over the bog-track of the Frosses where hidden waters
Lurk beneath the moss to choke you, or over the deep-pitted pathless
Boulders of the Long Mountain, or by Loughgiel's
Impenetrable elms, we are lost, Patrick.....
who will cry to you over Moyle's whirlpool patterns, cry
"Holy youth, walk among us and take your
Humble throne in the unchristened hearts"

Forward again and Columba of Derry passed by in 563 AD. With his twelve followers they travelled across to Argyll and up the coast to Iona. Here they set up a great missionary centre whose disciples carried the

Peace of Christ all over Britain and far beyond across Europe. Ireland was indeed the "land of saints and scholars". Once again many centuries later we have to decide which sort of Ireland is to prevail. As Ted Gordon's ringing lines challenge us in the Dalriada School song:

"Once to the north Christ's beacon light
Raised in Columba's hand
Amid the pagan dark to blaze
and triumph o'er the night;
As we your ancient glories praise,
Proud of our native strand,
We will uplift your splendid name in all men's sight."

Life Through Death

At Corrymeela you will see part of St. Francis' prayer engraved on the glass door at the entrance of the Croi. Later on in his prayer is the phrase: "It is in dying that we are born to eternal life" or as Jesus said "Whoever tries to gain his own life will lose it; whoever loses his life for my sake will gain it". What do these words mean for us? Here are two verbal pictures that may help.

There is a district on the edge of Liverpool called Neatherton. Until some years ago it was a quiet middle class suburb. At the centre was a very large Anglican Parish Church known as Christ Church. It had a huge nave and extensive ante rooms. As in so many other places after the war a lot of people moved out elsewhere and support for the church diminished and the whole district began to change, new housing programmes developed and the needs of the people who were there were very different, and this huge church, built for another age, seemed to be finished.

Fortunately in the crisis those in charge began to see new possibilities and challenges. Of course there were those who could not let the past go and wanted to soldier on regardless, but the others persisted. The church premises were restructured in order to respond to the new programmme. Part of the old church was preserved for worship, a library was planned and a recreation area for all sorts of activities. In addition, a self-service canteen was provided which served as a "drop in" centre and a daily meeting place for all sorts of groups as well as lonely individuals.

Recently I called there to see a young man, Michael Healy, whom I had met at Corrymeela and who was at that time a member of the staff. What a vibrant place it had become with all sorts of people from round about involved. I had lunch in the canteen with the staff who were holding their weekly meeting with all the clergy in the area, to plan for the coming week. Here indeed was "Life out of Death".

The other picture is a more personal one. It is about Osric and Nancy Spence from Melbourne, where he was a partner in an architects' firm. They had arrived in Corrymeela in 1976 and served as volunteer workers for a year. Here they made an unforgettable contribution. They used their personal skills in a most acceptable way, but in addition they had that priceless gift of being able to relate to and be accepted by young adults. Indeed in just a few months they became a very vital part of the Corrymeela family not only at Ballycastle but far beyond.

Why had they come? Well they had four grown-up children and shortly before they decided to travel to these islands, Rosemary, their 20 year old daughter had been tragically killed in a car crash. This journey, with this serving ministry at Corrymeela and elsewhere, was their response to the terrible pain, grief and loss they had suffered. In other words they decided not to stay at home and cling to the past, but to go out in love and service to others in need. Periods of similar service have taken them to Papua New Guinea and South India, as well as in the use of their home in Melbourne. Elizabeth Kuebler Ross sums it all up: "Hang on to what you have and you are lost. Let go and do the necessary dying and a richer fuller life will be given you".

A Mustard Seed

In June 1965 a group of some 40-50 people entered the Lounge at Corrymeela. It was a Saturday afternoon and the purchase of the premises had just been completed. This meeting had been called to express our gratitude and also to dedicate ourselves and the house to the work of Christian reconciliation throughout the country. It was not a very impressive event and perhaps a little self-conscious, as even then we stressed informality and also none of us were at all sure how it would all work out. This was indeed the very first Corrymeela event and somehow it almost took us by surprise, as the building itself was undergoing some long overdue renovations, and much obviously needed to be done before it would be fully functional. If I remember rightly I don't think there were even enough chairs to go round and some had to stand. I mention this because it seemed so much a non-event with no press and no television coverage. Yet it was a first step and something had happened.

The Gospel reading in the short worship included several short parables from Luke with these words: "If you then, who are evil, know how to give good gifts to your children, how much more will your Father who is in heaven give good gifts to those who ask him". A brief address followed with these sentences: "God is saying just that to us today: 'Have more faith in me, understand the sort of God I am. If you want a place where people can come together to know me better, where they can think about my world and my purpose  for it, a place where my followers can come together, especially those from different parts of my broken body and learn to trust each other, if you want that, I want it infinitely more'. Let us try to see what he would have this place be, the role it can play in the life of this country, a place of training and meeting, of peace and renewal and of challenge and response".

Looking back and trying to recall our feelings that day, I believe that some lines written by Norman Richardson specially for the first Corrymeela Summerfest in 1981 catch the spirit and hope of that time:-

> *Grow like a mustard seed, starting very small:*
> *Grow into the finest of trees, big and strong and tall.*
> *Kingdom of God, small as you now may be,*
> *Grow in us, rise through us, just like the mustard tree.*
> *Grow through all the earth, healing despair and pain;*
> *Kingdom like a mustard seed, bring us hope again.*

Strange Goings-On At Windsor Park

Not very far from where I live is the famous international football ground, Windsor Park. Many strange things have happened there, but nothing more strange than what I'm going to tell you. Some years ago, it may have been before the War, a group of young people decided they would arrange a most unusual match, and all the money would go to charity. They invited the Linfield Team and a Team selected from different rugby clubs to play a game. The match started with each team playing the game according to its own rules. The rugby players would handle the ball and try to score tries while the footballers would only kick the ball and try to score goals. Can't you imagine what it was like! It was quite funny for a short time, but it soon became confused, as one side tried to kick the ball over the bar while the other tried to get it under. Of course it became very difficult for the referee, and some of the players began to get just a little bit annoyed. Then they began to get angry. No longer was there any fun in it and there was no point nor purpose in continuing the match.

So at half time they had a conference and decided that it could not go on in this way. They carefully mixed the teams, some rugby and some football players on each side. Next they arranged rules that were acceptable to both sides and included some rules from each game and then they started to play again. Only this time it was completely different. They played very well together and discovered a lot about each other, for example, some rugby players could kick very well and some footballers were very good at catching the ball. They had a lot of fun and the spectators enjoyed it all greatly. The secret was, that in spite of their differences they found many things that they could do together and many skills they each had. Of course there had to be some giving and taking, some sacrifices on each side. But it really proved worth while, because each side discovered that they had far more things in common than differences.

I am sure you can see what I'm getting at. This match is really a picture of what is going on in our country. Each side wants to play only by its rules and they feel that the other side should accept them. The thing we've got to learn is, just like the players, that, we all, Catholics and Protestants have a vast number of things in common. Like those players we must be willing to go on to the field and begin to play together. Of course it has its risks, as everything worthwhile has, but it is the only way forward.

I remember one of the first schools' programmes we had at Corrymeela. Four classes of 12 year olds, two Catholic and two Protestant came to have a Geography Field Week. At first they were shy and afraid. But soon they were talking together, then studying and playing together. After they returned to Belfast one of the boys came to my home to ask when could they all return. He described how marvellous it had been and added: "At first I was afraid and thought there would be fighting, but it was not like that at all: we discovered they were just like us".

Fellow Travellers

One of the most interesting tasks I have had in Corrymeela through the years has been to travel abroad and tell of the work of our Community. This has taken me to many places in Europe and beyond. One of the most memorable was the trip to Lausanne in Switzerland in February 1973 to take part in the Week of Prayer for Christian Unity. Kathleen was with me and we were also joined by Father Tony Farquhar, who was at that time one of the Catholic Chaplains at Queen's University. He was later to become Auxiliary Bishop in the Diocese of Down and Connor, a position which he still holds.

This was an unforgettable experience for us all: a very full programme, very expertly organised, radio and television interviews, visits to different parishes in the Canton, several very large meetings, marvellous hospitality and a very sympathetic response to our story. I do not remember very much of what we tried to say, as we sought to explain the problems in Ireland and what Corrymeela was attempting to do. In retrospect I don't think that mattered very much, but rather the fact that we were together, travelling, speaking and staying together. It was that simple fact that made the impact. Indeed many people commented on that. Somehow this visible being together was more important than our words.

There is, however, another highlight of that tour that I will always treasure. One afternoon we had a pause in our very busy programme and our most thoughtful hosts decided that we needed a break, so they took us away up from the city into the snow-capped mountains and through a quiet peaceful landscape until we arrived at a village called Romain Moitier. We got out of the car and our hosts led us to a beautiful Romanesque Church which they thought would be of interest to us. No sooner had we entered the foyer than we began to realise why they had brought us to this place. On the wall immediately facing us, as we entered, there was a large map of Northern Europe. Ireland on the edge of Europe was marked out with a red circle. Across Holland, Belgium, France, Germany and Switzerland certain places were underlined. As we studied it, we could see that it was in fact the story of the Irish Missionaries of the Celtic period from the 5th to 9th Centuries who had journeyed from their various centres in Ireland. We can think for example of Columbanus who studied at the monastery in Bangor and later set out and established Christian communities in many parts of Europe. Then one of his followers, St. Gall, made a profound and lasting impression on Switzerland. You may guess how moved we were to learn that this Christian centre in Romain

Moitier had been founded by Irish missionaries. Then Ireland was described as "the land of saints and scholars" and the Irish were known as the great missionary race.

In the silence we thought about it and above all about the irony of our visit. Here we were centuries later, respresenting the Catholic and Protestant traditions, coming to try to explain the division and tragedy of our same Ireland in the centuries between. Before we left, we stood together with joined hands in the Sanctuary and said the Lord's Prayer, and prayed that through the healing of the Spirit our land would become once again "the land of saints and scholars".

The Tree Of Life

I still retain after many years a most vivid memory of the first weeks I spent in an Italian prison camp. It was in the middle of the summer and in very miserable accommodation, with small bivvy tents which gave scant cover from either the great heat or the rain. Food and water were very scarce, sanitation was primitive and the open field overcrowded. In addition, morale was low and the future uncertain. There was, however, one redeeming feature about the camp, and that was the great thickly-leaved sycamore tree at one of the corners in our square-shaped prison campo. This great tree was to become the camp's meeting place.

Here prisoners could gather together in the shade and talk, or have music or a discussion or hear the latest news, very mysteriously passed on to us from its source, a hidden radio. Under the tree, camp meetings took place to transmit information and orders from our "hosts". Here also prisoners gathered regularly for worship and prayer. To us all, the tree became a place of meeting, of community, of encouragement and support, and of humour and hope.

Now whenever I go into the Croi at Corrymeela, I am always reminded of that tree in Italy under which we used to meet. Because the dominant symbol inside the building is a tree, beautifully worked on linen with coloured embroidery, and set in a three-part sliding screen. The artist, Liza Andrews, based it on Revelation 22 v 2, which describes how the tree is planted beside the river of the water of life, flowing from the throne of God and "the leaves of the tree are for the healing of the nations". I always think what a wonderful sign the tree is of Christian Community. Here is unity and diversity, seen in the relationship between the trunk, the branches, the fruit and the leaves - some 300 of them, embroidered in a simple pattern by people from all over the world.

The Croi is a very special place in Corrymeela. The name itself means "the Heart", so this place lies right at the centre of the Community's life, both physically and spiritually. It is an open place in which all the different groups on site with all sorts of different needs, and coming from different places and traditions, meet together to pray.

Whenever I enter the Croi and look at the tree, my mind goes back to that camp with the great sycamore above and around, because again it seems to me that the whole of life is here. As I sit, I think of all those who come through the year: the politicians, the school teachers and the

and community leaders with their young people, the different clergy and theologians, those who come to face together the political, religious, and social divisions that create conflict, the many young adults, hurt and trapped by unemployment, having a low opinion of themselves and exploited by the sectarianism around them. In addition the many others who are the victims of a divided society: those whose men are in jail, those who are single parents, those who have been bereaved in the killings.

But this is also a place of challenge for those who seek to give and serve and who want things to change. Those who know that this is the place where Christ is met--in all these different people, and where his healing, forgiveness and peace are freely given to those who ask for them.

Canoeing Round Cape Horn

Canoeing is very popular at Corrymeela and many young people have learned the skills and been able to venture on the open sea. Colin Craig, the Centre Director, has done many exciting and interesting trips around the North Coast and further afield. However in 1987 he decided to do something special which had never been done before. With two friends he planned to canoe round Cape Horn, and so they set up the Cape Horn Expedition. Now if you look at a large scale map of this area, you will see that it is not just a sharp point, but rather a large mass of islands right round the Cape. Thus to circumnavigate the point they had to do a journey of 300 miles, weaving their way through the islands and at one point crossing 30 miles of open sea.

While it was a most exciting adventure, at the same time it demanded much planning and organisation. The starting place was Porto Williams and it took several plane stops and changes to reach it. In addition their equipment of 3 Sea Tiger canoes, food, paddles, tent, stoves, fuel bottles, and medical kit had to be crated and sent off some weeks in advance to arrive there in time. Many difficulties and disappointments had to be faced and overcome, before, at length, on the 3rd January 1988 they set out hoping to complete the journey within the month when the weather was still suitable. They had to face many hazards of wind, wave, storm, stretches of seaweed, and constant change of weather, as well as many events that were unpredictable. For example that awful morning on 15th January when they woke up to discover that one of their canoes had been swept out to sea and seemingly lost. After a herculean struggle with the wind they were able to recover it and go on their way. It was a hard journey with little respite right to the end, as the final ten miles were almost the most difficult they had to cover, to make their arrival on the 28th January.

It was a splendid achievement and demanded the greatest concentration as well as constant determination and dedication. The purpose of the Expedition was twofold: First to travel by this route which had never been done before. Second by gifts and sponsorship to raise support for Corrymeela and the National Childrens' Homes. For this achievement Colin was awarded the Winston Churchill Fellowship.

That certainly was some journey, and as I thought about it I realised that it presents a working model for all those who work for peace in Ireland, calling for the same qualities: intelligent preparation, understanding team work, sustained enthusiasm and the dedication that is willing to take risks.

"No easy path shall bring us to our goal,
But iron sacrifice of body, mind and soul".

The Cross Of Nails

If you walk down the entrance foyer at Corrymeela you will see a striking silver cross. It is mounted on a black velvet back-cloth. Look closely and you will see that the cross is made of three huge nails, two diagonally across and one perpendicular. It was presented to Corrymeela away back in 1974 and was the gift of Coventry Cathedral. Of course there is quite a story behind this.

During the early part of the Second World War a great number of cities in these islands were very heavily bombed by the Luftwaffe and, of course, Belfast got its share at Easter 1941. In November of the same year there was a specially heavy attack on Coventry and the whole centre of the city was devastated, including the ancient 13th Century cathedral, which was reduced to rubble. Shortly after, one of the Cathedral staff began to clear up the debris. Casually he picked up three of the ancient nails that had held the original roof beams in place. As he played around with them he discovered he could make a simple cross, but putting two alongside each other, the heads at each end. Then he placed the other nail at right

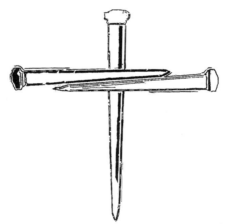

angles across them. So the Cross of Nails came into being. Immediately it became a sign of hope and resurrection out of the rubble and destruction, a sign of renewal and promise for the future and a symbol of life out of death.

In this they believed that they had been given a sign about the future of the building, that it should become a place of reconciliation. Action followed after the war. In the ruins with the help of a group of young

Germans a reconciliation centre was established. Appropriately these young people came from Dresden which also had been devastated by Allied bombers in 1945. Just after the end of the war a group of young people from Coventry travelled to Dresden and helped to rebuild a badly bombed hospital.

As the new cathedral began to take shape in Coventry, the vision of peace grew with it. A net-work, "The Cross of Nails Centres", began to take off and rapidly gave encouragement and generous support to peace projects all over the world. It was a great inspiration to us in Corrymeela when in 1973 Canon Dammers came over to Corrymeela and presented us with the Cross of Nails. Later they announced that they wanted to do even more and so they organised a world wide appeal to support our work in Ireland.

This appeal was very well organised and as a result we were able to build the much needed Coventry House, which has added to the work of our community in providing well equipped and comfortable quarters for our residential team. A great number of volunteers and field workers through the years were and are grateful to Coventry for this very real and practical sign of support.

To me, every time I go into this lovely house I think of the marvellous generosity of the Coventry team and of the people all over the world who have provided this here for us in Ireland, and I realise the reality of Christian solidarity and of Paul's words: "When one member suffers the others suffer with it."

Madame Tussaud's

Most of the tourists visiting London sooner or later arrive at Madame Tussaud's wax work exhibition. Of course, there are a multitude of items to see according to your taste: some hurry away immediately to the Chamber of Horrors, and others like to walk around and see the models of famous people both past and present. There is one other place I would mention and that is the Hall of Mirrors.

Whenever you enter you are immediately confronted with a great variety of mirrors of all shapes. As you go round with your friends you will have a few good laughs at each other, as you learn how each mirror distorts your body in some way or another. One will make you look tall and thin with a long head, body and legs, while another shows your body like a barrel and your head like a small balloon. In another you'll have a huge body with tiny legs and head and another just the opposite. It is all good fun if not very complimentary. However, while you recognise yourself in each mirror it is quite a relief to see yourself back to normal again. It is also quite a comfort to remember, that in spite of all the distortions, you find that all your body, arms, legs and head are in each mirror.

Frequently at Corrymeela there is discussion about the differences between the various churches and I always think of the Hall of Mirrors. It is often suggested that in some churches some of the elements are missing, just as if an arm or leg were missing in a body. If, however, we look back through Church History we can see that it is a sort of Hall of Mirrors in which the Christian Faith sees itself now with this and now with that part exaggerated and even distorted. But remember that all the parts are there in each case. For example in each you will find the Bible, the Ministry, Worship, the Sacraments, Proclamation of the Gospel and, of course, Christ crucified and risen.

It is rather like an orchestra. When the musician composes, he has the same choice of time and harmony, as well as the same range of instruments as any other composer and yet how different and varied the results. Some composers will emphasise the strings more than the wind, others the brass above the percussion. But they are all there.

So it is vital in all our discussions to remember the things we have in common while not forgetting the differences. One of my friends was for a time a missionary in Indonesia. There were very few other missionaries there. He did discover one other quite near him. He turned out to be a Roman Catholic. Before they met my friend wondered how they would get on. Would there be arguments and disagreements? But when they did meet they found that it did not turn out like that at all. Very soon they discovered they had so much in common, not only in the conditions and living, but in their belief and practice and how they sought to share their faith with the people in the country. So they became very close friends, supporting and encouraging each other. That relationship profoundly changed the attitude of my friend to the other tradition.

Setting Each Other Free

One of the loveliest places I have ever visited is Florence. I went there with a party of students in the sixties. This beautiful city seems to preserve the very life and spirit of the Renaissance, with most of the majestic buildings and palaces of that remarkable period intact. It all remains almost unchanged with the narrow streets bright in the strong persistent sunshine, and a skyline with the timeless Duomo and Giotto's Tower, the Uffizi and Vecchio Palaces. One almost expects to meet Galileo or Donatello or even Savonarola hurrying past.

The outstanding memory I have, however, of an all-too-short visit was of Michelangelo's sculpture of David. It was almost like one of those "stills" on a television programme, when the figure on the screen is suddenly "frozen" for a minute or two, and then in a flash, back "live" again. It was as if somehow Michelangelo had seen David in the massive block of Carerra marble and released him from it. That set me thinking, because that surely is what is happening all the time in our relationships with each other.

For example a school teacher by sheer enthusiasm can release the latent interest and talent in a reluctuant pupil or a parent can inspire a child to incredible achievement. In each person there is so much waiting to be released: things they might attempt, roles they might play, needs they might meet. Indeed, putting it in another way, the Spirit of Christ is already in each of us but is so often deeply buried, forgotten, and ignored, at the same time waiting to be released. Then on the other hand hidden fears, resentments, prejudices, and hatreds are thwarting, binding and imprisoning so many lives. Though waiting to be set free, we are all powerless to release ourselves.

Robin Boyd in his book, "Ireland", points us towards the answer. The situation is like that of two handcuffed prisoners, each unable to set himself free. Then one of them discovers a hacksaw blade and thinks: "This will enable me to cut through my fetters". But he is unable to use it, for his hands are bound. Then he realizes: "We can use it on each other's fetters, we can set each other free". Indeed that is something we have learned in our Corrymeela programmes, that the Spirit works through you in releasing me, because when you share with me your story, you are helping me to be set free from my fears and prejudices and creating trust, understanding and healing.

Bishop John Taylor describes the Holy Spirit as the "Go-Between God", the one who works through one person to release the Christ in the other person. Listen to these lines written from prison by Richard McIlkenny, one of the Birmingham Six:

You were a prisoner in me, Lord,
And I could not set you free.
I had forgotten you were there, Lord,
Lying deep within my soul.
You took the scales from off my eyes, Lord,
And filled me with your love,
Through those you did bring to me
Like angels from above.

Labels

From time to time groups of Senior Citizens come to spend a few days at Corrymeela. Sister Vincentia from the local Cross and Passion Convent used to come and help with such groups. One particular week there was a party of Pensioners from the Shankill Road district, a strongly Protestant part of the city.

That week the weather was not very good, so the old people spent most of the time indoors, watching films, playing games or having concerts or just talking about their lives and friends and, of course, enjoying many cups of tea. Helpers play a most important role in making sure that no one is left out.

Anyway, as it happened, Sister Vincentia spent a lot of her time talking to one pensioner, called Tommy, from the Shankill. Towards the end of the week someone said to him: "Tommy ye're gettin' on very well with that wee nun". Tommy immediately rounded on her and said: "That's not a nun, she's the District Nurse". Nevertheless something very important had happened. A real personal relationship had taken place and Tommy's idea of a nun completely transformed. He had been able to see beyond the label to the real caring friendly person behind it.

That little incident points to one of the great tragedies of our society - the use of labels and stereotypes that obliterate the real person behind them. It is a temptation we all face, whether we do it in a blunt crude way or use a more subtle and suggestive method. Indeed we can do it unconsciously. I remember the first German soldier I saw during the war. It was at a petrol point near Tobruk in North Africa. As I looked at him, scrutinizing each detail, I began to realize how taken in I had been by the stereotypes of propaganda. I had expected him to look ruthless and hard, a typical haughty jack-booted Nazi. But this man was not like that at all, as he leant against the wing of his desert truck. He was so relaxed, with his peak cap aslant and his sand-covered jacket open, casually chatting and laughing and smoking his cigarette. He just seemed like any of us.

Moreover, this process is going on all the time in our relationships. It is so easy to label people and in doing so to write them off: "Harry is impossible to work with", or "She is a pain in the neck", or "a bigot", or "a fanatic". Or it can be done socially: "Jim really does not count for much", or "He is a lightweight", or "She has a poor background", or "He is a drunk", or "a womaniser".

The tragic thing is, when you label people you de-humanise them, just like in a Nazi concentration camp, where there were no names, only numbers. Jesus always saw people as people, not types or classes. Think of the folk he re-humanised and whose dignity he restored: the woman taken in adultery, the miserable little tax collector or the terrorist beside him on the cross.

Once I visited Boys' Town in Omaha Nebraska, created by Father Flannigan and made famous by Spencer Tracy's film. There is a little statue at the entrance depicting a small girl struggling along, trying to carry a ragged boy on her shoulders. Father Flannigan suggests that he is too heavy for her. She replies: "He's not heavy, Father, he's my brother".

Every Crisis Is An Opportunity

Since its earliest days Corrymeela has had many close links with the Samaritans and some members have worked in their programmes. When one thinks of all this organisation has achieved, the name of the founder Chad Varah is never far away. He pioneered this vital service because he was convinced, that whatever the situation was, one should try to do something in response to it. It was never good enough simply to deplore or lament.

For example away back in the 50's there was a public outcry about the horror comics available to children and young people, followed by protests and denunciations. Varah, however, knew that such complaints were not enough and something more had to be done. It was futile to ban the comics. Children wanted to read and this need had to be met. So he gathered together a group of experts: those who understood children's interests, those skilled in commercial art, and those who knew about publication and promotion. The end result was the appearance of those interesting and exciting weeklies: the "Eagle", "Swift, "Robin" and "Girl". All of these immediately captured very wide support among young people. In other words Varah proved the truth, that behind every crisis there is an opportunity. It is interesting to know that the Chinese ideogram for crisis has two characters in it: one meaning "break-down" and the other "opportunity".

Never before has the word "crisis" been so often on people's lips. Daily we are informed about national crisis, political crisis, food crisis and personal crisis. These all demand decision and choice. Our personal lives, the future of our society and the destiny of the nations depend on choices. Arnold Toynbee, the famous historian, has analysed the rise and fall of nineteen different cultures and how they came and went. The process, in each case, he maintains, has the form of Challenge and Response. Survival depends on the depth of the response made to the challenge of the time.

Political leaders in our own country have from time to time posed the same challenges for us. Do you remember: "What sort of an Ulster do you want?" A vast number of people have not honestly faced that question. Some just shut it out of their minds and ignore it. Yet there is so much that can be done and is waiting to be done here. After all, political decisions and choices cannot be separated from our everyday life, from our hopes and fears, from the courage and determination we have, and the first steps we are willing to take. The future depends in the end not on the big dramatic events, but rather on the small initiatives, the risks taken and the willingness to speak out and to take a plunge.

There is an ancient graveyard somewhere in England and in it is a gravestone which dates back to the time of the Civil War in 1641. The stone was erected in memory of the man who built the church and below his name these words are engraved:

"Here Lies One Whose Great Achievement Was
To Do The Best Of Things In The Worst Of Times".

Thanksgiving

"O LORD REMEMBER
Not only the men and women of good-will but also those of ill-will.
But do not remember all the suffering they have inflicted on us,
Remember the fruits we bought, thanks to this suffering,
Our comradeship, our loyalty, our humility,
The courage, the generosity, the greatness of heart
which has grown out of all this,
And when they come to judgement,
Let all the fruits that we have borne be their forgiveness".

This prayer was found on a piece of wrapping paper, near the body of a dead child in Ravensbruck Nazi Concentration Camp where 92,000 women and children died.

This prayer is surely one of the most amazing ever written and it challenges us to consider what Thanksgiving is. In the Bible we are frequently told that we should give thanks for all things. "Always and for everything give thanks in the name of our Lord Jesus Christ", is how Paul puts it in Ephesians. Indeed this theme of thanksgiving runs right through the Bible and psychotherapists would agree heartily. G. K. Chesterton, as so often, puts it in a sentence: "The atheist is the saddest person in the world, for when he wants to give thanks, he has no one to thank".

Of course, there are a vast number of things we can be thankful for without any difficulty: the beauty of the world around us, the love and support of our friends, all the attractive and lovely things we experience in music, painting and literature, and all the comforts and privileges we enjoy every day.

But we must look at the other side of life. What are we to say about thanksgiving, where these other very different things show up, the hurts, the pain and loss, the disappointments, the shattered dreams, broken relationships and impaired health. It is so easy to be glib here and pull out the smooth answers, especially if we have not had to contend with such realities. The first thing we have to do is to recognise that we work on a very small canvas. Our perspective is so narrow and limited, as Paul said: "Here we see through a glass darkly". "We only know in part". This life is indeed a life of shadows.

To me one of the central parts of the Christian Faith is what the Church has traditionally called 'the Eucharist' - 'the Giving Thanks'. Yet when you think about it, what a tragic story it begins with, as in the Service we remember one who suffered the cruellest and most unjust death imaginable, and in so doing shattered the hopes, dreams and indeed the lives and the faith of multitudes of those he had met. Those two broken disillusioned disciples on the Emmaeus Road summed it up for everyone: "But we had hoped that he would be the one who was going to set Israel free". Then there is that amazing twist in the story. Suddenly, incredibly the broken-hearted disciples discovered that he was alive and risen and with them for always in all the tragedy and pain. Here a new dimension had broken in, that not only transformed their lives but all human history and experience. That is why that at the very centre of Christian Faith and practice there is the Eucharist - 'the Thanksgiving'.

Chancing Your Arm

When you next visit Dublin, you ought to go to the Chapter House at St. Patrick's Cathedral. If you look at the door you will see that a hole has been cut or hacked in it. The story of this goes back a very long time. It was in the year 1492 which was the same year as Columbus' journey to America.

There were two great families in Ireland, the Ormonds and the Kildares, and for generations they had feuded and fought with each other. In this particular year they were fighting in Dublin and the Earl of Ormond and his followers were put on the defensive and decided to take refuge in the security of the Chapter House, which was a very solid building. Gerald Fitzgerald, the Earl of Kildare, surrounded the House and prepared for a long seige.

As time passed, Kildare had some time to think and the more he thought the more he came to believe this endless feuding and killing was utterly foolish and indeed sad. After all, both sides had so much in common. For example they both shared the same country, worshipped in the same church, and believed in the same God. So he shouted out to Ormond on the other side of the door that he should come out, and to quote his own words: "he should receive no villanie". It is easy for us to understand that Ormond was not convinced.

Kildare, however, refused to leave it there. He saw that something more than words was needed. So he took up his spear and cut and hacked a hole in the door, and when it was large enough, thrust his hand and then his arm through. His hand was open and Ormond was very moved by this brave gesture and grasped the hand. The door was opened and the two men embraced each other and the family feud was at an end. That noble gesture of Kildare is the origin of the expression "chancing one's arm".

Kildare's action changed the whole situation, as it broke the deadlock and opened the way to new possibilities and changes that forced people to change their minds and begin to think in a new way. Perhaps the most important thing about it was its unexpectedness. This took people off their guard and broke down their old stereotype image of "the enemy" and the only way to respond.

But was that not how Jesus lived and taught all through his short life? The old way, and it is still very much with us, was "an eye for an eye and a tooth for a tooth". Jesus tells us that we are to forgive our enemies, to turn the other cheek and walk the second mile, and not only did he say that but he lived it out.

I think especially of two individuals who witnessed the dying of Christ on the Cross - the Roman Centurian and the terrorist criminal. No doubt they had both seen it all before - the various techniques to break the victim's spirit and de-humanise him: the torture, the wounds, the abuse and insults. But this man was completely different. He displayed no bitterness or resentment but rather a complete concern for those round about: his mother, his disciples and above all for his tormenters. "Father, forgive them for they know not what they do." This completely shatttered and transformed these two men.

So at the last a soldier and a terrorist were the first to recognise who he really was!

Our Dog

I have always thought there is something special about dogs. I know it is difficult to say what it is, so the best thing I can do is to describe our dog, Kerry. We are not quite sure what her family background is, but we do know that she has a strong Collie look and colouring. She has a very striking coat of light brown and white fur, with a long fine head and large flappy ears and a very intelligent eye. I should say she has only one eye and was born that way, but it seems to make little difference to her activities.

She is a very gentle dog and loves our grandchildren and altogether behaves very well. Of course, like us all, she has her faults, which come out when I take her for a walk. Usually she trots very demurely by my side, but what a change takes place when she sees a cat on the horizon. I don't know what gets into her but she suddenly changes, and barking furiously, tugs at the lead to be let free. There is another thing which puzzles me about her and that is, for some reason she cannot stand postmen or bin-men and really gets very upset when she sets eyes on them. Otherwise she lives a very quiet and orderly life.

I suppose the great thing in her life is going to Corrymeela. It is quite amazing, that when we travel by car, she sits very quietly in the back, mostly asleep. But when we get about a mile from the town of Ballycastle, she's up on her feet, her tail wagging with anticipation and gentle growls of pleasure. I suppose she thinks of the marvellous walks along the beach and the sticks thrown into the waves for her to retrieve and a refreshing plunge in the salt water. Sometimes she takes off after low flying seagulls, but they seem to play games with her, as they entice her to chase them, and when she has nearly caught them, they just flap their wings and majestically sweep out of her reach. I am sure that animals have a sense of humour.

47

She, like some other dogs, has a very important contribution to make to Corrymeela. Let me explain. Very often parents arrive at the centre with their children and they are very shy and not quite sure just what it is like. So whenever they arrive off the bus and leave their cases in their bedrooms, they come down to the lounge feeling strange, because they have not been before and know very few people. Then in walks Kerry. She doesn't need to be introduced. She goes up to the children, wagging her tail and putting her paw up to be shaken. Very quickly the children gather round her and suddenly the ice is broken and everybody begins to chat and the evening meal is ready.

I like the Dog's Prayer by Piero Scanziani:

O Lord of all creatures,
Make man, as faithful to other men as I am to him.
Make him as loving to his family and friends as I am to him.

Give him, O Lord, an easy and spontaneous smile,
Easy and spontaneous as when I wag my tail.
May he be as readily grateful as I am quick to lick his hand.

Grant him patience equal to mine,
When I await his return without complaining.
Give him my courage,
My readiness to sacrifice all for him,
Even life itself.

Keep for him the youthfulness of my heart,
The cheerfulness of my thoughts.

O Lord of all creatures,
As I am truly a dog,
Grant that he may always be truly a man.

The Search For Meaning

Some years ago I read a remarkable book written on this theme. The author was a Viennese Professor, Viktor Frankl. The book is very special to me, not because the author is a leading psychiatrist who has founded his own school of interpretation, rather to me the interest is in the background to the book, the setting in which it had been written. Frankl is Jewish and like so many of his faith, was imprisoned for three years in the infamous Auschwitz Concentration Camp. When he eventually got his freedom, he discovered that his whole family had been wiped out. It was against this terrible background, that he worked out his own thinking.

The first section of the book describes something of the unbelievable conditions with which they had to contend. One passage sums up the whole depersonalising process: 'Each prisoner was nothing but a number. On admission to Auschwitz all documents and personal possessions were removed. The authorities were only interested in a prisoner's number. These were usually tatoo'd on the skin. Moreover any guard who wanted to make a charge against a prisoner glanced at his number - he was never asked his name. No effort was spared to brutalise the prisoner, with the daily routine of violence, blows, kicks, shouts, obscenities and indescribable cruelty. In this way existence descended to the animal level and life became cheap, and human suffering aroused less and less feeling.'

The other part of the book describes Frankl's response which can be summarised in three points:-

First, man is not just the victim of his surroundings. He has a choice, and there were those in the camp who were able to choose inner freedom.

Second, the all importance of inner and personal values in surviving. He describes how some of them were able to win through. In some cases it was because of their religious faith, for others it was through their creative urge, and others were sustained by loving relationships. In his case it was due to the love of his wife, (even though he was to learn of her death before his release), that he was able to survive.

Thirdly in a word, those survived who were able to find meaning to life even in such a place. As Nietzsche said: 'He who has a WHY - a purpose to live for, can bear almost any HOW.'

This principle,
however, is vital far beyond the
extremities of a concentration camp. Perhaps it is
here that Corrymeela's real work is being done. I
can think of many ways of how it happens. For
example there are those young adults who have had
a good education and secure prospects for the future.
Then the various encounters as Corrymeela open their
minds to new and unthought of possibilties. Those
who discover that they really want to work with young
people, or with handicapped, or perhaps work overseas
and are prepared to take the risk of changing course.

The real crunch though is the large groups who feel they cannot cope
with our competitive society and become depressed, seeing themselves as
worthless with no contribution to make. This to me is a vital issue for all
who are concerned for the future - just to direct whatever influence and
power we have to enable these young people to discover that they are of
worth and have a contribution to make. Perhaps the greatest tribute ever
paid to Corrymeela was by a young lad who had been in constant trouble
with the police and had been in prison several times. He said, "This is the
first place where anyone has ever bothered about me". Now he has a job
and has happily settled down.

Mother Teresa At Corrymeela

Of course this was a very memorable and exciting day at Ballycastle. After all it is not every day that a real live saint drops in. Indeed that was the right expression as one of her journeys was by helicopter. The field used for her departure was owned by an elder in the Presbyterian Church and he summed it up with a typical flash of North Antrim wit: "Man there'll be a fine crop of spuds in this field next season". Certainly it was an unforgettable day for us all. Although she had had a most exhausting flight from Venezuela by Madrid and London, she put us all at ease by her readiness to accept any requests made to her and also graciously coped with much that was unscheduled, because so many people wanted to speak to her. We were profoundly impressed by the way she related to each person and each group, many of whom were deeply distressed by the continued violence and the problems they had to face.

Kathleen describes one such group, a bus load of Belfast mothers returning from a prison visit to Magilligan. 'They were exhausted, the children were whining, while they waited in small dim television upper room. The door opened and Mother Teresa stood there studying each face silently. Then she spoke "You mothers", she said "are very privileged". Astonishment registered on every face. "You are able", she continued, "to share the pain of Our Lady. You have to watch your dearest ones suffer and can do nothing about it". Then glancing at the wistful peaky faces of the children, she added, "And you must smile five times a day - it is good for the children".'

Very thoughtfully Doug Baker had planned for her to meet the 'back room people', who did the cleaning and cooking and could not hear her speak in the marquee. Very beautifully she spoke about the importance of what they were doing and the privilege of service and how central it was in the life of our Lord.

We both had the great experience of having lunch with her. Again we recall how much she put us all at ease by her outgoing friendliness and gentleness. I asked her about leprosy and she told me of the many thousands looked after by her Order, but there was no sense of boasting but rather very obvious sadness and pain that she could not do more, as she added, "But there are five million lepers still in the world". We noticed that though she kept talking continuously throughout the meal, she kept on eating until she had finished all on her plate. No food could ever be wasted.

Of course none of us will ever forget her talk and the way she spoke and the compassion coming through in everything she said. Her words were so simple, so real and so compelling. Here was one who spoke about the love of Christ which profoundly touched our hearts. Indeed, somehow, we all knew that she had the right to use them, because her whole life was a living parable of those words and, "something beautiful for God".

Having A Fixed Point

A very popular excursion at Corrymeela in summer time is a trip to Rathlin Island. There is all the excitement of a sea voyage across the Moyle Water with unforgettable views of the famous columns of Fair Head rising at right angles six hundred feet out of the sea. To the west lie the white limestone cliffs of Kenbane Head and beyond, the headlands of the Causeway and in the distance Inishowen and the Hills of Donegal. Following this there is all the adventure of exploring the island with its four lakes, its hills, beaches, and famous bird haven as well as the lighthouses.

Although the passage across to the harbour in Church Bay is only seven and a half miles, it is not an easy one. In fact it has been described as one of the most dangerous strips of water in all Europe. Early history and legend seem to support that view. It has been called the Cauldron of Brecain and it was here that the Grandson of Niall of the Nine Hostages lost his life along with 50 Curraghs and their crews. The tide in the race flows 9 hours in flood and only 3 in ebb. Part of the reason for this may be explained by the Irish name for this sound which is Sloch-na-marra, which means "the Hollow of the Sea", indicating how deep it is.

Jack Coyle was for many years one of the regular boat-men and has crossed this strip of sea times without number. I remember one day when we were returning from a trip to the island, asking him if he was ever afraid in the many times he had done the journey. He replied that he was always afraid "until I get her lined up with the harbour" and then he could relax, as he was in the calmer waters and well on the way home.

It is true that in every part of life we need our fixed points, not only in places of risk but also in making our decisions and deciding how we should live our lives, the sort of society we want and indeed the sort of world we desire. There is a phrase that is very much used these days when people are discussing any political or social or moral issue, and it is the frequent accusation that he or she "is moving the goal posts", i.e. they are bending the rules to suit what they want at that particular time. But that is just a recipe for disaster wherever it is tried. Yet it is a great temptation, as so many react against rules and authority.

Jesus did not begin with rules and regulations. He began at the other end with people and where they were. In fact he started with relationships, which are, after all, what life is really about. When he was asked which was the greatest commandment, he replied "You shall love the Lord your God with all your heart.....The second is, You shall love your neighbour as yourself. There is no other commandment greater than these".

In the end life is not about commandments, or systems, or political or social ideologies. It is about faith, and trust and love. Professor Herbert Butterfield ends his famous book, "Christianity and History" with this sentence:

"We can do worse than remember a principle which
both gives us a firm rock and
leaves us the maximum elasticity for our minds - the principle:
Hold to Christ and for the rest be totally uncommitted."

Learning To Speak Our Language

One of the most trying and yet amusing things about going abroad is attempting to speak the language. I recall very vividly being with a party of Queen's students in the Rhineland. Most of them knew little German and on the journey over had been rather feverishly trying to grasp a few words and sentences from the little phrase books they had bought on the boat. Others, more foreseeing, had done a few lessons with records. You see we had to live with German families and we realised how difficult it would be, if we could not utter even a few words of their language.

Of course our early attempts led to a lot of confusion and not a little amusement. One of our party was a medical student and when asked by his host what he intended to be, he replied: "I am going to eat a doctor". Another girl student was asked what she would prefer for breakfast and she startled her host by replying: "I would like to become a sausage". Perhaps the most unforgettable was of the student who asked his host if he could "rave in the kitchen, as the bathroom was occupied". (The German word for shaving is "razieren", while "razen" is to rave).

We soon realised that if we really wanted to get to know and understand the Germans we had to learn their language. Only in this way could we be able to know what they felt, the sort of people they were and their hopes and fears. Otherwise our relationship could not be very close and in a real way we would remain strangers to each other.

This has made me understand how important words are and how powerless we would be without them. It is by words that we communicate with each other. The truth is that "every man is an island" and if we hope to survive we have to be able to give and receive messages or signs from each other.

I am sure that this is what Christmas really means. Before Christ came, people really knew little about God. True they had some ideas but often they were confused and vague. This led to frequent misunderstanding and even contradiction. Their ideas were very limited and his character was often a great mystery to them. We could almost say they did not understand his language.

But God did not leave it there. He spoke to us. He communicated with us. As John wrote at the beginning of the Gospel: "The Word became a human being and, full of grace and truth, lived among us". Jesus is God's sign, his message, his word to us. Or we could put it another way-in Jesus, God speaks our language.

That is what Christmas is all about and why it is such a wonderful celebration. I like the phrase of C. S. Lewis:

"There is nothing now between us and Him".

The Church At The Bridge

In May 1985 Kathleen and I had the great pleasure of a trip to what was then the East German Republic. For us the high point of our trip was our visit to the city of Dresden on the River Elbe. Dresden has been called the Venice of the West and it is famous for its art, music, architecture, poetry and of course its china. Our host was a German pastor called Christoph Ziemer, who very kindly showed us round the city and on Sunday asked me to take part in the service in his Church. It is a very ancient and well known building right in the heart of the city and close to the Elbe, though perhaps it is even better known for its famous Boys' Choir which travels all over the world. After the service Christoph showed us round the Church and told us something about its history. It dates away back to the Middle Ages and is called the Church of the Cross. (Kreuzkirche)

To me the most memorable thing was the ancient symbol or, as we would say, logo, which was very simply a cross against the background of a bridge. Then we learnt that there had always been a very close tie between the church and the bridge across the Elbe very close at hand. At the beginning the Church had helped to raise money to construct the bridge. This was very important, as the city began to develop on both banks of the river and naturally the people found it very slow and laborious to cross in a ferry.

Time passed and often there were uncertain periods of unrest and conflict. At such times the Church was able to keep the bridge open and so allow ordinary everyday life to continue. Again when it got into a state of decay, the Church was at hand to have it repaired and indeed improved. So it came to be known as 'The Church at the Bridge' and that is how it got its logo.

'The Church at the Bridge', surely we could not have a better picture of what the Church is meant to be and its job in the world to be at the bridge, to keep it open and in good repair. The bridge stands at the place of division and separation, at the boundary and the frontier, the place of misunderstanding, prejudice and fear, but it is also a place of new horizons, new possibilities, new hopes and new relationships. John Mackay of Princeton sums it all up: "The Church should be at the place where life is lived most closely to man's need and God's purpose".

Doing The Unexpected

A very remarkable man, Elias Chacour, was one of the special speakers at the Corrymeela Summerfest in July 1989. He is a pastor of the ancient Melkite Church in a small village called Ibullin in North Galilee. The Melkites are a very ancient branch of the Church. The members are Palestinian Christians and through the centuries they have survived by holding on to the simple orthodox teachings of the Early Church. When Elias first arrived in Ibullin he was shattered, because he discovered not only the incredible bitterness and feuds among the members, but also that some deeply resented his arrival, as his predecessor had apparently robbed the people. He decided that he had to do something really drastic.

So Palm Sunday arrived, and though the Church was packed, the atmosphere of hostility destroyed any sense of spiritual reality. The singing was pathetic and his attempt at a sermon was even worse, and the people barely disguised their boredom and hostility. Then he did the utterly unexpected thing, as the people rose for the Benediction. 'I swiftly dropped my hand and strode toward the open doors at the back. I drew shut the huge double-doors. From my pocket I pulled a thick chain, laced it through the handles and fastened it firmly with a padlock. Turning to the congregation I took a deep breath.

"Sitting in this Church does not make you a Christian...You are a people divided. You argue and hate each other, gossip and spread malicious lies...Surely your religion is false. If you can't love your brother whom you have seen, how can you love God whom you have not seen?...For many months I have tried to unite you. I've failed, because I am only a man. But there is someone else who can bring you together in true unity. His name is Jesus Christ. He is the one who gives you power to forgive. So now I will be quiet and allow Him to give you that power. If you will not forgive, we will stay locked in here. You can kill each other and I'll provide your funerals gratis".

Silence hung. Tight-lipped, fists clenched, everyone glared at me, if carved from stone. I waited. With agonizing slowness, the minutes passed. Three minutes...five minutes...ten. Someone was standing up. Abu Mouhib (the ring-leader) rose and faced the congregation, his head bowed, remorse shining in his eyes. "I am sorry" he faltered. "I am the worst of you all. I've hated even my own brothers, hated them so much that I wanted to kill them. More than any of you I need forgiveness". and then he turned to me. "Can you forgive me, too, Abuna?" "Come here", I replied. He came and we greeted each other with the kiss of peace. "Of course I can forgive you", I said, "Now go and greet your brothers".'

Everyone in Northern Ireland should read "Blood Brothers". It is a compelling account of this Palestinian Christian and his struggle to reconcile Jews and Palestinians. Here are no smooth or easy options. It is an uncomfortable book for us. Chacour came from a deeply Christian home where his parents prayed and longed for the healing of the hatred - a hope shattered again and again by events. He, like his

fellow Palestinians, has had to work through the alternatives of quietism, prayer and waiting, or the temptation of the bomb and the bullet. Is there not another way? The book describes his efforts to work out this third way.

Anyone Can Speak To The King

There is a strange sentence in the first chapter of Esther. It reads: "And the seven princes of Persia, who saw the King's face". Do you know what this meant? It meant that only very special people such as the seven princes were allowed to look at the King. Indeed in much more modern times it was rather like Japan, where only very special people were able to look at the Emperor. This meant that when he passed by your home or your street all the curtains had to be pulled across so that no one could see him.

That reminded me of an incident that a News Reel Photographer, called Ronnie Noble, described in a book he wrote about his experiences mostly during the last war. He was sent to cover a tour that King George VI was making round the East Coast Defences of England, to meet some of the soldiers and inspect the various barriers that had been erected against the expected invasion. It was a two-day journey with many stops, and there was quite a long procession of cars with other camera men, as well as press and radio, and in addition the various people that have to accompany the King. Unfortunately Noble's car was very far back and at each stop he had to go quite a distance to where the Royal party had halted, and so each time he arrived just too late as the party was about to move on. Eventually he made a supreme effort to get up to the King's party. But just as he was

getting close to where the King was standing, an official moved across and barred his way, so that he could not go any nearer. Ronnie Noble got a little bit annoyed and said: "But I want to speak to the King". Again the official refused to let him past. The King, however, was near at hand and heard Noble's request and coming across he looked at him and said "Anyone can speak to the King". He then asked him where he would like him to stand and he was able to take a marvellous shot of the King right against the East Coast Wall.

But so many keep on making the same mistake when they think about God. They think still that God is only interested in very special and important people or those who belong to a particular group or race or class or indeed, just in the good or religious. Jesus came to put that right and to tell us and show us that God's love and concern are for all, no matter who or what they are.

It is very chastening to ask yourself that if Jesus were to come to Belfast in the flesh, who would he relate to and where would he go? If you look at the Gospels you'll get some of the answers. He is described as "a friend of tax collectors and other outcasts". He numbered prostitutes among his friends. In Matthew he identified himself with the hungry, the thirsty, the stranger, the naked, the sick and the prisoner. These are the people he has special concern for and to whom he is specially near.

The Painting Class

Frank Wright is a Corrymeela Member and one of his contributions has been to create an interest in painting - and this is for everybody who wishes to take part, whether they have done it before or not. I will never forget the day I joined his class. It was a lovely warm clear day and the class had gathered on the narrow coast road just below Corrymeela and overlooking the little beach locally known as McGuire's Strand.

When I joined them they were not painting, although they had their easels set up and paints prepared. In fact they were standing around watching Sam McLernon, a well known artist at work, painting this part of the North Coast. He had very graciously agreed that this group of beginners could watch him in action. Sam was absorbed in his art, as gradually he produced on his canvas a wide-angled sketch of Ballycastle Bay. It outlined the town and the headland to Kenbane Head and on to the open sea. In the foreground the beach wall with spurs of dark brown rocks reaching out into the white foamed waves, and below, the light brown sands of the little beach.

It was fascinating to see Sam's picture develop, as his brush moved confidently across the canvas. In watching I began to feel something happening in myself. Many things I had never noticed before came to my mind, although I had passed along this very road times without number. I recognised the shadows cast by the wall across the sand, and the rocks darkening the water. I saw, as I had never before, the variety of colours across the sea, all the shades of blue and grey. As I looked up I felt ashamed that I had never grasped the wonder of the cloud formations with all their variety of shapes, texture and the interaction of light and shade.

In fact I began to see the things that had always been there, but to see them in a new way. We could say I became aware of them. This gift of awareness is one of the greatest of all human gifts and it is the supreme ability of the scientist, the poet, the artist, the philosopher and the ordinary person. It lies at the heart of all great scientific studies, as when the revolutionary concept of gravity comes to Newton, as he watches an apple fall to the ground. Or indeed to any one of us: when we fall in love or waken to the beauty of a piece of music or a picture, or in a tight corner experience the loyalty of a friend.

Above all, this is what authentic religious experience is about, whether it is Elijah in despair, or Moses at the Burning Bush, or Isaiah in the Temple or the two travellers on the Emmaus Road. Malcolm Muggeridge had a similar experience when making a television programme about Christ in the Holy Land:

"..a curious almost magical certainty seized me about Jesus.....
I became aware that there really had been a man,
Jesus, who was also God. I was conscious of his presence.
He really had spoken those sublime words. I heard them.
He really had died on a cross and risen from the dead.
Otherwise how was it possible for me to meet him as I did,
preaching on the hillside about how the meek inherit the earth
and the pure in heart see God, falling in step along the road
to Emmaeus?.....Thus he is alive.....Jesus is alive".

The Healing Of Memory

"On February 13th and 14th, 1945, Dresden, the great city of culture was destroyed. At least 35,000 were killed and many estimates are much higher, as there was no record of the vast refugee influx. In the Central Railway Station 16,000 lost their lives, 175,000 dwellings were destroyed, 40 hospitals, 35 schools, 75 cultural buildings and 27 churches". These were the cold clinical facts, as outlined in a church magazine. But who can describe the suffering and grief that still lives on after 40 years. The bombs were dropped in three Anglo-American raids.

You can appreciate something of what I felt, when I returned to Dresden in 1985 after 40 years, for I had been a prisoner there during the raids and worked as a YMCA Chaplain. I wondered what sort of a reception I would receive. I will never forget the welcome we received (Kathleen was with me) from Christof Ziemer, the Superintendent Pastor in the famous Kreuzkirche. On the Sunday he asked us to take part in the Eucharist. Kathleen read the scripture and I spoke of how I felt. I described honestly the hatred and bitterness of my fellow prisoners, because of what they had suffered in the forced marches from the East in the depth of winter. But I also spoke of how shattered the same prisoners were by the death and destruction wrought by the massive air raids and the subsequent fire storms or holocaust.

I went on to say that today we all met at the one table, shared the one bread and wine, and were forgiven and reconciled by the one Lord. I quoted Paul: "For Christ is our peace, who has broken down the wall of hatred between us". Somehow I felt that those words had been given to me and that I was not speaking only for myself but also for my fellow prisoners whom I represented. We shared the peace of Christ and I gave Christof an Irish Cross and he gave me a simple coloured glass plaque that had a silhouette of the Destruction of Dresden and above it a rainbow, the sign of God's covenant of grace and forgiveness.

The sequel again was unforgettable. We were taken to the Opera and saw Karl von Weber's, "Der Freischutz", which had been playing 40 years ago on the night of the bombing. During the interval the lady sitting next to Kathleen began to talk to her. She said that she and her husband had been at the service in the Kreuzkirche and recognised us. She went on to explain how her husband had been in the city on the night of the raids. Though he was a 16 year old, he was in the army. On that night, however, his mother, his 6 year old brother and grandparents had been killed. As a result he vowed that he would never forgive the British and Americans for what they had done. The lights went down and the Opera continued and when the end came, we missed them and Kathleen told me what the lady had said. I felt very sad that we had not been able to talk.

Outside, people were crowding out of the Opera, and cars were setting off, when suddenly this man rushed across the road and through the traffic. He ran over to me and grasped my hand, there were tears in his eyes and he simply said to me: "Now I can forgive", and ran back across the road and vanished into the night.

Finding Out Who You Are

Some years ago there was a very popular film called "The secret life of Walter Mitty" and the main part was beautifully played by Danny Kaye, the film star who did so much for the United Nations Childrens' cause. Though it was made many years ago, a great number of people still remember it. The reason was, of course, that everyone could recognise themselves and their own experience in it. The theme was about a young adult growing up and imagining himself in all sorts of very dramatic and dangerous situations and playing the great hero role.

For example, he imagined a great day of triumph with a vast crowd thronging the streets, waving flags and throwing streamers, everywhere the noise of shouting, cheering and band music. Then the climax as the victorious general arrives in the packed city centre, to be greeted with ear splitting applause. He dismounts from his worthy steed and slowly climbs to the huge platform, smiling and waving to the crowds. Of course Mitty was the General. The scene changes and this time it is a vast Olympic stadium with again a massive crowd of wildly excited spectators. The athletes are poised for the 100 metres. The starter lifts his pistol. Sudden quiet descends, as the athletes crouch down and settle on their "marks". The thunder of the pistol and they're off. One athlete with his head lifted and body bent forward edges away from the others inch by inch and finally hurls himself at the tape to win the Olympic Crown. Of course again it was Walter Mitty. The scene changes dramatically and we are at the seaside and the beach is crowded with bathers. Then a sudden cry goes up for help and one brave young man with a body like a Greek God plunges in, and after a titanic struggle with the elements, returns with the beautiful blond who had gone out too far. Of course again it is our gallant Walter Mitty.

This is all great fun and we can recognise it as normal at a certain stage of life. The difficulty is when we get stuck at this point and our development is arrested. This is very often due to the expectations of other people and the vested interests of those who have their own ideas about what we ought to be. It is not a new problem and everybody has to face it. Wise people from the past have left several basic ideas which can help us.

There were the Greek thinkers whose great theme was: "Man, know yourself". This meant that we should learn to think for ourselves and about ourselves and not let other people do that for us. That is, we should not just swallow other people's ideas and opinions, we should make up our own minds. As Paul wrote to the people in Rome: "Don't let the world

around you squeeze you into its own mould".
Then there were the Romans and they said:
"Man, control yourself". Self-discipline
was the key to all their remarkable
achievements in ruling, building and
law making. Then there is the
Christian thing: "Give yourself" to
something or someone infinitely
greater than yourself. Jesus tells us
that we are to lose our lives in order
to find them. He often spoke of the
half-hearted, those who had not
considered the cost and turned
back, or those who split their
loyalty.

Remember the remark of Bill
Shankley, the famous Liverpool
Football Manager, and recently
quoted by Dr George Carey, the
newly installed Archbishop of
Canterbury: "Football is not just a matter of life
and death: it is more important!". That is the sort of commitment to Christ
that is called for today and through which we will find out who we really
are.

The Loneliness Of A Marathon Runner

Michael Earle was Centre Director at Corrymeela for five years and left last summer to return to New Zealand, where he with Anne and the family had lived before they came here. Whenever I think of Michael several pictures come to my mind: there were those well planned programmes, when we had visitors from outside Ireland who wished to know about the Centre's work and the general situation in the country; there was the memorable trip to Taize; the very imaginative 'Two Traditions' week-end in the spring of 1990 and most vividly Michael's running the Belfast Marathon in 1989. I may say I was mildly surprised, when I learnt he was to do it. I knew that he had been a top-class athlete in his student days, but that was over 20 years ago!

Nonetheless he trained for the 26 miles plus ordeal and not only survived it, but was able to write an article describing what it was like from the inside, as it were, and, at the same time, provide a sort of tourist-style commentary on the different areas the runners passed through. He tells of "the stern unflinching expressions on the young faces (of the soldiers) on the Falls Road. Dehumanised and unaccepted in this part of the city, constantly on the alert, suspicious of every move, seen as the enemy agents of a foreign power in Ireland". In contrast the local cheering and clapping for anyone from Corrymeela - 'Corrymeela, I've been there'. The paradox - so full of friendliness, yet so full of hatred and mistrust as well". On into another area "past the Loyalist mural on a gable wall of King William crossing the Boyne on a white stallion, and we were into Protestant territory".

Later, the pressure increases "Pass the 18 mile mark in 3 hours. Haven't hit 'the runners' wall' yet, but still feel sore in the legs". Then at 21 miles "Keep plodding on. Think I can now finish the run, so long as I do not stop. My legs want to." 23 miles "Hey, I can make it. Just keep going-- forget the soreness. Just keep moving on....." Later 'Only 2 miles, no more hills', shouts the race judge. Past the 26 mile mark and on to the final stretch---"a wonderful crowd of Corrymeela supporters. I remember all their cheery faces - the tunnel of people at the finishing line - 4 hours 32 minutes---the legs just don't want to work once I stopped. I feel numb and glad that everybody from Corrymeela had made it".

It had been a personal challenge and a milestone to remember for a long time. It had been widely sponsored and over £1000 for Corrymeela. We were all proud of Michael and the other Corrymeela runners. It was a noble effort and indeed showed them to be worthy followers in the ancient Marathon tradition with its great courage, determination and endurance.

But surely the Belfast Marathon is a symbol of something more: a picture of the society that Northern Ireland can become, where the emphasis is not on success or rivalry, but rather on running side by side, sharing the ordeals and struggles, supporting and encouraging each other: a picture of a true community where there is no "us" or "them", but all of us running together in confidence and hope: a whisper, an annunciation of what the Good Lord wants our society to become!

Life Is Commitment

I will never forget a remarkable week I spent in June 1963. It started when my brother, John, and I travelled to Gartin about 10 miles from Letterkenny in Donegal and from there across the sea to Iona on the West Coast of Scotland. We both had gone to Donegal to take part in a service at the birth-place of St. Columba near Gartin Lake, to celebrate the 14th Centenary of his departure from Ireland. With his 12 companions he set sail from Derry in a curragh, travelling along the Antrim Coast, then across the North Channel and up to Dunadd in Argyll and across to Iona.

Our journey to Iona from Ireland was much more prosaic and roundabout, as we had to travel by steamer up the Clyde to Glasgow, followed by a long car journey and two more ferries and a bus run across Mull. Of course that week in June was a time of almost continuous celebration and ecumenical services. Iona was the centre of news, as many groups descended on the small island, as well as some notable people such as the Prime Minister, Harold Macmillan, and the Archbishop of Canterbury, Michael Ramsey. The weather was delectable and the island at its best and an absolute gift for the cameras of the television companies and press who had swarmed over from the mainland to cover this event.

I suppose it was by way of contrast from all this activity, that my most vivid memory is of a pleasant walk John and I had across the island away from all the bustle and noise. We set out from the Abbey and past the Reilig Odhrain, the burial place of the Scottish Kings, including Duncan and Macbeth, as well as Irish and Norwegian royals. Over to the North we could see Dun I-the 400 foot hill, a marvellous vantage point for the surrounding Hebridian Islands and the mountains in Mull across the Sound of Iona. Next we enjoyed the easy walk across the Machair - a sandy plain, the garden of the island, where cultivation is possible. After this the rough track sloped gently down to the sea where we found a very pleasantly secluded cove with the waves gently lapping on the shore.

This was the Port of the Curragh, for it was here that Columba and his crew landed. Tradition says that he first climbed the hill to make sure that Ireland could not be seen and then they buried their boat deep in the sand. There was to be no returning to his beloved Ireland. They had committed themselves to a new venture and a new life. Of course it is difficult to separate fact from fiction, but the story certainly is in keeping with all Columba did and his decisive life-style. So through this decision Iona became a great centre of Christian Community, Worship, Learning and Mission to the mainland and its influence was to reach far beyond these islands and spread out across Europe.

It is not only fascinating but inspiring to meditate on the results of that commitment of Columba to Iona and what came from it, not only in those early centuries but continuing right through to modern times and the foundation of the Iona Community of today with its emphasis on the unity and totality of all life: work and worship, spirit and matter and God in all things - all so much part of the Celtic and Columban way of life.

George MacLeod, the Founder of the Iona Community and so much the heir of the Columban tradition, catches the spirit in these lines:

> *Invisible we see you. Christ beneath us.*
> *With earthly eyes we see beneath us stones and*
> *dust and dross, fit subjects*
> *for the analyst's table.*
> *But with the eye of faith, we know You uphold.*
> *In You all things consist and hang together:*
> > *The very atom is light energy*
> > *The grass is vibrant*
> > *The rocks pulsate.*
> *All is in flux; turn but a stone and an angel moves.*
> *Underneath are the everlasting arms.*
> *Unknowable we know You, Christ beneath us.*

What About A Wee Dander?

Words are fascinating and some of them have very interesting stories behind them. I believe the word 'dander' is a good example. I have often used it without trying to understand just what it means. I suppose we could say that it means going on a very casual stroll, with no particular purpose or place in mind. Sometime ago, however, a friend suggested to me that it might be related to the word 'saunter'. It's true that 'dander' and 'saunter' do sound a little bit like each other.

Anyway the word 'saunter' has a very historical background. It dates back to the time of the Crusades in the 12th Century. At that time there was a very strong feeling of anger and dismay in England and France that the Holy Land was in the hands of infidel Turks, who were Mohammedan. So the Crusaders called for volunteers who would join them and drive the Turks out of Jerusalem, the Holy City. A great number of people in England believed that this was a very noble cause and if they were too old or unfit to go themselves they sent gifts of money and goods to support those who were willing to go.

Then a strange thing began to happen. Some of those who went round collecting, enjoyed it so much that they decided to put off travelling. However they continued walking around shouting "La sainte Terre-La sainte Terre" (The Holy Land). Remember, of course, that in those days French was very widely spoken in England. Naturally they would talk a lot about the journey, all the dangers they would meet and, indeed, the wonderful things they would do when they got there to free Jerusalem. Of course they enjoyed all this and the people praised them and they still rattled their collecting boxes and kept on shouting 'La sainte Terre'. But they stayed on at home and did not set out, until at length they did not go at all. So they came to be called the "Saunterers" - "sainte-terre-ers". Those who talked and boasted but never set out-just dandered round the country.

We may smile at them, but it is so easy to be like them: to have big ideas and endless discussions, but leave it to a committee or until the next meeting to make decisions. The real people are those who make up their minds, choose and decide, and take a risk, those people who put on their boots and get out on the road!

The Place Where No Birds Sing

In May 1985 Kathleen and I were invited to attend a gathering in East Berlin. It brought together representatives from all the countries that had been involved in the Second World War. It was unusual in that it was not called together for discussion or debate or passing resolutions. The purpose of the East German Churches who planned it, was that we should just meet as Christians to listen to each other's stories, share our hopes and our prayers for the future.

The visit lasted for four days and the one experience that I remember above all others was the visit to Sachsenhausen Concentration Camp about 20 kilometres from Berlin. Our bus took us to the very pleasant little town of Oranienburg. It was a very warm day and we were glad to walk out along a cool shaded avenue and stretch our legs.

Our stroll ended as we came to large gates and at what looked like the entrance to a public park with people and children in a holiday mood coming in and out. Suddenly with quite a mental jolt I grasped that this was the Camp itself. As we entered I was surprised to notice how extensive it was, and from the diagram at the entrance I could see that it was laid out in a tidy triangle. It was about the size of the Balmoral Show grounds.

I will not attempt to describe in detail the terrible apparatus of repression, torture, and execution. The very words in themselves were ominous: "the Cages", "the Gallows", and "the Ovens". Our hosts were very sensitive to our feelings and organised a pilgrimage round seven Stations, or focal points in the Camp. The first was "the Gate". We stood round in reverent silence. Then one of the German Christians made a brief statement: "This was one of the first concentration camps that the Nazis installed.....More than 200,000 passed through these gates, less that 100,000 ever came out". Then a pause and a prayer: "I beg God and you the members of this meeting to forgive my people".

So many thoughts crowded into my mind as we moved round and just the sheer horror at what had happened here in this place. We were told that since those grim days no birds sang in the trees nearby. Again it was shattering to remember that these deeds had been done by citizens of probably the most cultured nation in the world, and in our time just a few decades ago. Yet could we outsiders absolve ourselves? Had not our people played a part in creating the right conditions for the rise of the Nazi creed?

There is one place I'll always remember: "the Cages". In these the most important and the most hated prisoners were confined. They were called on to suffer terrible cruelties. In one of them I saw a plaque with a photograph of Pastor Martin Niemoller telling that he was imprisoned there in 1938 as Hitler's personal prisoner. One day another imprisoned pastor, called Gruber, saw Niemoller coming under escort. They were not allowed to speak, but Gruber quickly wrote one word in Latin on the sand. VIVAT. He lives. Christ lives. In the midst of incredible cruelty and death there was life and hope! I remembered St John's Gospel:

"The light shines on in the dark, and the darkness has never quenched it".

The Village

A great institution in the life of Northern Ireland is "The Village" and I am always happy that my early days were lived in such an environment. In my case it was Dunmurry which in the 20's and 30's was very much aware of itself as "The Village" and the five mile space between itself and Belfast.

Anyway it was a marvellous setting in which to grow up where there was so much colour, life and drama in everyday life, in addition to an abundance of local characters and challenging activities. Compared with this current technological age, those days were basic and uncomplicated. We had to find or improvise our entertainment without the help of Television and Radio which was just beginning. The Railway was the main means of transport, as few people owned cars. My own father, as the Presbyterian Minister never drove a car and did all his visitation on foot or bicycle. I can vividly recall the advent of electricity in our village and how we delighted in playing with the switches.

There were no Supermarkets and all the shops were locally owned and staffed. You were not sent to the Grocer's but to "Jimmy Gray's" for a pound of sugar or butter. I can still vividly recall the various names of the shopkeepers and tradesmen. There was Murtie Magee - the Butcher, Johnny Porter - the Plumber, Andy Bruce - the Barber, Wiltie Agnew - the Blacksmith, Tib Kerr - the Taximan, and "Patch-in-the-eye" - the Road Mender. On those rare, very rare occasions when we had any money to spend, it was to Mosie Hunter's that we repaired. She was a little old black shawled woman with very thick glasses and a perpetual cold in the nose. Here we could buy "Gub-Stoppers", "Kayly Suckers", "Black Balls" and of course the timeless Wrigley's "Chewing Gum".

One of the main culture shocks for me was moving to the Public Elementary School from a very small private establishment. Here the cane was the ultimate encouragement, and certainly the basics were well ground into us. Everyday life for the villagers was no idyllic utopia. With no Social Security and rampant unemployment, life was hard. TB was common and even as a child I was aware of malnutrition and poverty. Yet in spite of all, there was much that was not only commendable but at times inspiring. There was a real sense of identity and community expressed in the on-going social, sporting and religious activities. People did matter, and their occupation or lack of it, where they lived, as well as Christian names were all known. Generosity and mutual support were part of life.

One final memory sums it all up for me and that was Communion Sunday in Church. Of course, as a small boy, there was much that was beyond my understanding. I did, however, grasp the feeling of peace and expectancy among those present. Here, in a sense, the whole life of the village was present, here, surely, was the core of the community, where all met on common ground, as sons and daughters of the one Father, and in their brokenness and failure, needing the forgiveness and healing of the one Christ, and going out in the joy of the one Spirit. Indeed here I began to see those who were present, the gardener, the business man, the engine driver, the housewife, the farmer, the district nurse and the garage man in a new light.

When we partake of the living bread and the living vine, our triune
God.
Help us to know ourselves to have part in earth redeemed;
Help us to know ourselves to have part in the new life blood for the
world;
To cling together as branches of the vine,
To give both shade and refreshment to the world.
Help us all to be Thy healing spirit in the world
till all shall be pervaded.
So shall we freshly partake:
So shall we freely purvey:
So shall we freshly be Thy life of love
till Thou shalt come to judge.

Sydney Harbour

I have visited many harbours, but none compares with Sydney. It is so spacious and dramatic with the great Bridge spanning right across it and so many ships and so many mooring places that the whole city seems to be built right round it. We were only sight-seeing for a few hours and it was extremely warm, but we did cover a lot of ground; we saw the famous shell like Opera House, built right out on a little peninsula; we had our first trip in a hydrafoil, and a very bumpy and wet ride up to Manly Beach.

There is, however, one experience that does stay in my memory and that was the meal our hosts provided for us as a climax at the end of the day. The restaurant was at the top of a sky-scraping block right on the harbour. The unique feature about it was that it slowly revolved. As far as I recall it took about one hour to complete a single revolution. This meant that we were able to relax, enjoy our meal and at the same time have a delightful panorama of the different parts of the city and the harbour. It was an unforgettable end to a very special day. It all left us more grateful than we could say to our friends for their kindness and generosity.

When we came home I wrote an article about our trip, partly for our Corrymeela friends at home and partly for our Australian hosts. Alas, my writing is unreadable at times and when the article had been typed up and about to be sent out I discovered that there was one mistake. In a way it was very small, involving only one letter. The word REVOLVING had been replaced by the word REVOLTING, in my description of the restaurant. I wonder what my friends in Australia would have thought, if it had reached them! As far as I know it did not. At least they still write and visit us when they come over here.

Just one letter wrong, seemingly such a little thing and yet so

important. It reminded me of our prison camp in Italy. Escape was regarded as almost impossible and yet two of our prisoners somehow managed to get out of the camp and well away from the district. They had disguised themselves as Italian workers with suitable caps, jackets and trousers. All went very well until they came to a very busy road which they had to cross to get through to the Allied lines. Such roads were very carefully patrolled, and as they were about to cross, an Italian soldier challenged them to stop. They seemed to be getting clear when he looked down and noticed their boots. He recognised that they were not Italian and very soon the game was up and they were on their way back to the prison camp.

Small things are so important. In the early days of Corrymeela a mother came from Belfast with her children. She was very nervous and had not been away from home before and also was very uncertain about this strange place. Then a young American volunteer met her and gave her a great smile and helped to carry her bag to the bedroom. Later that mother was heard to say: "As soon as I came through the door I knew I was welcome".

The poet, Blake, puts it in a sentence:

"If you want to love your neighbour you must look at details".

Travelling Light

We had been on the road for several days and were weary with the strong late afternoon sun and the heavy bags strapped to our backs, and so we lay down for a brief rest by the dusty road-side. It was early May 1945 and we were prisoners-of-war trying to get through the German and Russian lines to the Allies. We knew that the war was nearly over, but the situation around us was very fluid and we were very unsure what was happening. We had escaped from the medieval castle in Saxony and knew that we were on or close to the Czech border and also that we were going in the right direction, but very uncertain as to what lay ahead of us, as the day wore on to evening. We were very fortunate at a town called Teplitz to arrive just as a small battle had finished.

So we had called a stop to take stock of our position and our best course of action. We all agreed that we would have to lighten our bags and keep only those things that were essential for our journey. As prisoners of three years we had accumulated many souvenirs including books and diaries as well as spare clothes and food from Red Cross parcels to keep us going, but now the moment of choice had come.

Soon the grass verge was covered with discarded books, tins of food and extra boots, shirts and socks. That was a difficult choice for each of us to make and many a cherished book was left by the roadside. We knew, however, that if we were to keep on

the road and get through, all our energy and strength would be needed.

I have never forgotten that day and the painful choices we had to make. In ordinary life it is just as important to stop from time to time and weigh up our priorities and avoid the temptation to carry too much baggage. I remember the advice of the writer to the Hebrews "Let us lay aside every weight and the sin which clings so closely" and Jesus also tells us that we are to travel light.

Several years ago we had the great privilege of a visit from Mother Teresa of Calcutta at Corrymeela. Of course she made a profound impression on all who met and heard her. One thing I specially remember and it is a very simple one. Several of us accompanied her to a helicopter that had been chartered to take her to a very important meeting in Dublin. I stood and watched her waiting, this frail little woman who had travelled from across the world to be with us. There she was, dressed in a very simple cotton habit and carrying all her possessions in a small plastic bag. Yet I felt that she was the richest of us all, because as Paul wrote in Corinthians "as having nothing yet possessing all things".

Be Patient With Me
God Isn't Finished With Me Yet

Do you like caterpillars? Some people do and others do not. Of course, they are creepy and crawly things and a lot of people can't stand that. Whenever they move they go very slowly and they don't walk, they wriggle along. Their long bodies just seem to be a series of rings and they move in and out almost like an accordian. They have 13 rings with 3 pairs of true legs and 5 pairs of claspers which can also serve as legs. They are very particular about their food and will only eat lettuce or cabbage, and of these they eat a lot.

However, the most amazing thing of all about a caterpiller is the way it changes really into something else. The beginning of the change is when it becomes a chrysalis, which is a sort of case that encloses the caterpillar. When this happens it rests for a long time and then the miracle takes place. The chrysalis breaks apart and a new creature is there - so completely different. It is a butterfly - one of the most beautiful creatures of all with its great coloured wings. It no longer slides along the ground but flies across the fields and gardens, darting here and there from one flower to another, bringing colour life and joy to all who see it.

This transformation is, to me, one of the most wonderful in all nature and I have often thought that it points far beyond itself. It is a sign of dynamic qualities not only of nature but also human nature, and that is to change, not only physically but also in personality and character.

This change, however, comes from outside us. It is not a do-it-yourself process. It is here that so many people miss the point and keep on trying to work it all out themselves. Look, however, at the New Testament and indeed at human history and you will readily see how all sorts of different characters were changed. Peter, Matthew, Mary Magdalene, Paul and later on Augustine, Luther, Wesley and on into our own time. The key word for them all is relationship. In some way or another each was related to Jesus. Sometimes it was a very sudden encounter, for others it was a gradual awareness, and again for many it was in and out of uncertainty until finally they knew. Throughout my own journey I have had many uncertainties and doubts, but somehow, this relationship has been there from early on in my life. At times it has been challenging and rebuking, at others supporting and encouraging. Sometimes it is very strong and sure, at others uncertain and weak. Nonetheless, through all the ups and downs - it has always been there.

These lines of Camus sum it all up for me:-

Don't walk before me - I may not follow.
Don't walk behind me - I may not lead.
Just walk beside me - and be my friend.

Easter Day Pilgrimage

Remembering 25 years of Corrymeela.

This was a very special day coming at the end of a reunion week-end that brought together former staff, volunteers and members, many of whom had travelled long distances to be present. The USA, Finland, Germany and Switzerland were all represented as well as England and Scotland. It was a great time for renewing friendships, sharing memories and news as well as getting up to date about Corrymeela today.

Easter Day brought it all to a climax, when we tried to express our gratitude by making a Pilgrimage round the various places in Corrymeela that reminded us of the different stages of the journey and also pointed us to the future. Colin Craig, our Centre Director, with the present Volunteers led the way, carrying long standards bearing yellow pennants that fluttered in the strong wind, the hopes of a clear sunny day not being realised. The Singers turned out in force to lead the music for the many Members and Friends with children taking part.

The first Station and starting place was, very appropriately, at the Cottages, the site of the early work-camps and the pioneer days. Here we recalled all the work: painting, plumbing, digging, carpentry and cooking; the fun and the laughter each day; the discussions and conversations; the vision, hope and the dawning faith. Against the background of surpassing beauty we gave thanks for the Guiding Hand that had led us and helped us survive 25 turbulent years.

Inspired by some of the chants from Iona and Taize we moved on to Station Two in the inner courtyard of the Village. This has been the setting of many of the youth programmes and a long list of other conferences, seminars, "Resource" and "Seed" groups, school and family groups and, of course, special times like Open Days and Summerfest. We remembered with gratitude many of the Field Workers and staff who had made their own special contribution.

Coventry House provided the third Station and here we thought of the marvellous support that has come from all over the world such as Coventry Cathedral, the London Corrymeela Link and the ongoing untiring efforts of the Link based in Reading and their efforts over 12 years. We remembered too, the help from Holland, Germany, America and Switzerland.

Station Four took us to the Memorial Playground. Here we thought of the pain, sorrow and loss of so many in our country including some of our own Members and Friends. We also remembered those of our Community who had completed this part of the journey.

The fifth Station took us to the cliff edge of the front lawn from which we looked out from Corrymeela to the wider world and at the same time thought of the future and what lay ahead seeing it in the light and promise of Easter Day. As we sang Sydney Carter's "Lord of the Dance" some of the young people joined hands and spontaneously broke into a dance - an inspired expression of what we felt, as we walked together into the future.

Finally in the Croi we re-affirmed our commitment to the work of reconciliation and "spreading the pollen of peace". Perhaps one remark passed between two Members as they walked together summed it all up. In response to the question: "What do you think of the weather?", the other person replied "Surely it is symbolic". In other words in our pilgrimage for healing and peace in this country, the going is never easy and at times is rough and hard. But still like the Pilgrims at Corrymeela we go on in faith and hope, remembering John Bunyan's lines:

Who would true valour see,
Let him come hither;
One here will constant be,
Come wind, come weather:

There's no discouragement
Shall make him once relent
His first avowed intent
To be a pilgrim.